THE OFFICIAL GUIDE TO AMERICAN FOOTBALL

NFL

DAVID BOSS AND JIM NATAL

TO GET THE BEST
FROM WATCHING AND
PLAYING THE GAME

HAMLYN

Designed by David Johnston

Published in 1989
by The Hamlyn Publishing Group Limited
a division of The Octopus Publishing Group,
Michelin House, 81 Fulham Road, London SW3 6RB

ISBN 0 600 56552 1

Produced by Mandarin Offset
Printed and bound in Hong Kong

Contents

The Game

The Players

American Football at a Glance

Football is a sport of contrasts. It has action on every play, then calm between plays as each team decides what to do next. Some football players are big and powerful, but others are small and fast. Brute strength often is required, but so is intelligence, agility, and skill. It can be a game of great complexity, especially at the professional level, yet the basics are easy to understand no matter who is playing.

One 11-man team has possession of the football. It is called the *offense* and it tries to advance down the field, by running with the ball or throwing it, and score points by crossing the *goal line* and getting into an area called the *end zone*. The other team (also with 11 players) is called the *defense*. It tries to stop the offensive team and make it give up possession of the ball. If the team with the ball does score, however, the offensive and defensive roles are reversed. And so on , back and forth, until all four quarters of the game have been played.

Football has all the action and excitement, subtleties and athletic grace of other popular sports, plus the intellectual challenge of a good game of chess. But most of all, football is fun – to watch and to play. And the more you know about it, the more fun it becomes.

The Ball

The unusual shape of the football makes the action of the sport unique. It is shaped to be carried, thrown, and kicked. Because of the football's shape, its bounces are unpredictable. A football is made of a pebble-grained leather skin stretched over an inflated rubber bladder. The official football of the National Football League measures approximately 11 to 11¼ inches long (end to end) and 21¼ to 21½ inches in circumference (around the middle), and weighs 14 to 15 ounces. There is a slight size, weight, and graphic variation among the footballs used by professionals and college and high school teams in the United States. At every NFL game, there are 24 footballs available, provided by the home team. An official checks all the balls prior to the game to make sure each is inflated correctly.

Yards and Downs

The yard is the unit of measure in football (1 yard = .9144 meter). The team on offense tries to advance the ball and gain "yardage" (numbers of yards). It gets four *downs*, or chances (numbered first through fourth in sequence), to try to go 10 yards and make a *first down*, thus achieving another series of four downs. If the offense fails to make the yardage necessary for a first down, or to score, the ball goes to the other team.

Officials

There are seven officials on the field to enforce rules, assess and signal penalties, and keep game time. Penalties are assessed in yards or downs—or both.

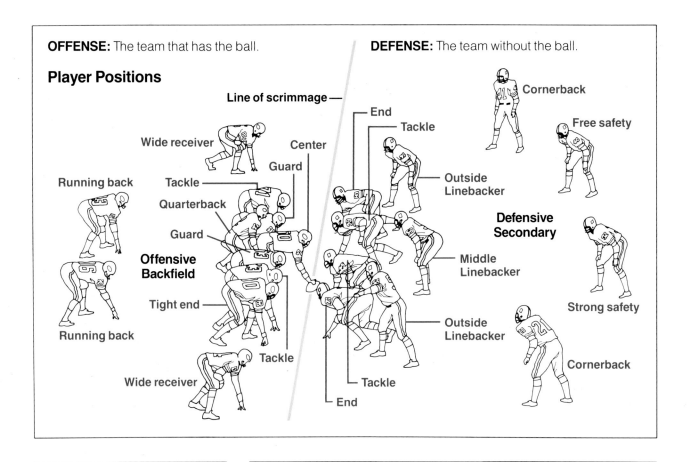

OFFENSE: The team that has the ball. **DEFENSE:** The team without the ball.

Player Positions

Line of scrimmage

Wide receiver
Center
Guard
Running back
Tackle
Quarterback
Guard
Offensive Backfield
Tight end
Running back
Tackle
Wide receiver

End
Tackle
Outside Linebacker
Defensive Secondary
Middle Linebacker
Outside Linebacker
Tackle
End

Cornerback
Free safety
Strong safety
Cornerback

Player Numbers

NFL players are numbered according to their positions:

- **1-19** Quarterbacks and kickers
- **20-49** Running backs and defensive backs
- **50-59** Centers and linebackers
- **60-79** Defensive and interior offensive linemen
- **80-89** Wide receivers and tight ends
- **90-99** Defensive linemen

Scoring

Touchdown	=	**6** points
Field goal	=	**3** points
Safety	=	**2** points
Extra point	=	**1** point

Game Time

Game	=	**60** minutes
Quarter	=	**15** minutes
Halftime	=	**15** minutes
Overtime period	=	**15** minutes
Time out	=	**110** seconds
Maximum time between plays	=	**45** seconds

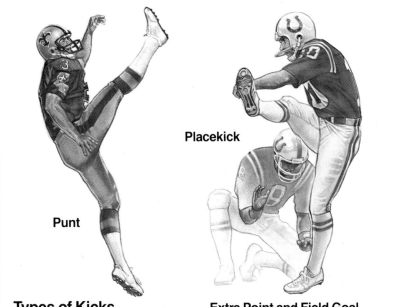

Punt

Placekick

Types of Kicks

Punt: The ball is kicked away to the other team, usually in fourth-down situations.

Kickoff: The ball is placed upright on a kicking tee and kicked to the other team, from the kicking team's 35-yard line, at the beginning of a half or after a touchdown or field goal.

Extra Point and Field Goal

The ball is snapped to a holder and kicked through the uprights of the goal post. Extra-point kicks follow touchdowns and are snapped from the 2-yard line and kicked from about the 10. Field goals may be attempted from anywhere on the field on any offensive down.

The Field

A regulation football field measures 120 yards long, 100 yards from *goal line* to goal line, with a 10-yard-deep *end zone* at either end. The field is 53 ⅓ yards wide (160 feet). Depending on the stadium, NFL fields have surfaces of natural grass or synthetic grass, such as AstroTurf. Special shoes are required for each surface. The weather has no effect on field conditions in indoor domed stadiums. On outdoor fields, however, rain, snow, wind, and freezing temperatures can critically affect the play on the field.

Team Benches

Each team is assigned a side of the field for its players. Team benches are located in the area between the 35-yard lines along each sideline, and 10 yards back from the sideline. Players are not allowed to leave this area during play except to go into the game.

Yard Lines/Field Numbers

The field is lined at five-yard intervals between the goal lines. Yard-line numbers appear every 10 yards, beginning at the 10 and running up to the 50 (also called the "midfield stripe") and then back down to the 10 again. An arrow pointing toward the nearest goal line is marked beside each number on either side of the 50.

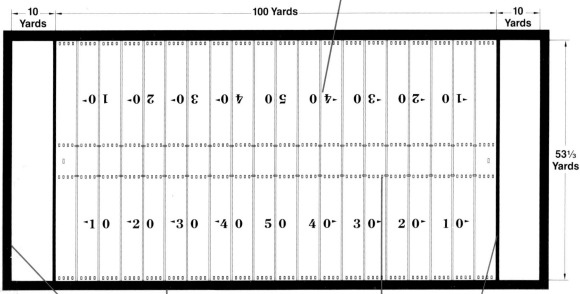

End Line

The end line is the line at the back of each end zone. It is parallel to, and 10 yards behind, the goal line. The goal posts are set on the center of each end line. Short, bright orange plastic pylons are located where the end lines meet the sidelines.

Sideline

Running the length of the field and bordering the field of play are the sidelines. Any ball or player going *on or outside* these lines is considered "out of bounds" (un-like soccer, where being on the boundary lines themselves still is considered in bounds).

Hashmarks

Hashmarks are short stripes set one yard apart between each yard-line stripe. They are located 70 feet 9 inches in from each sideline, aligned with the uprights of the goal posts. Hashmarks are used by game officials to *spot* (position) the ball after each play.

Goal Line

The goal line is a white field stripe that is twice as wide (eight inches) as any other stripe on the field. To score, a player must cross the goal line, or "break the plane of the goal," with the ball in his possession. Orange pylons also are located at the intersections of the goal lines and the sidelines.

Game Time

A football game is divided into four 15-minute *quarters*. The first and second quarters make up the game's *first half*, the second and third quarters the *second half*. There is a 15-minute intermission between the end of the second quarter and the start of the the third called "halftime" or, more simply, "the half." At halftime, the teams leave the field and go to their locker rooms, where they rest, attend to minor injuries and equipment problems, and discuss strategies for the second half. Both halves of the game begin with a kickoff. The winner of a pregame coin toss chooses whether to kick off or receive to begin the game, or which end of the field to defend. The team that loses the pregame coin toss gets its choice of kicking or receiving or of defending a particular end zone to start the second half. At the end of the first and third quarters, there are intervals of two minutes. At this time, the teams exchange directions on the field so that neither team maintains an advantage from prevailing weather conditions. The end of each quarter is signaled by the firing of a starter's gun. If the score is tied at the end of the regulation four quarters, a fifth 15-minute period, or *overtime*, is added to NFL regular-season games. Overtimes are played on a "sudden-death" basis—the first score of any kind wins the game. If neither team scores in the overtime, the game ends in a tie. Games cannot end in a tie during the NFL's "postseason" playoffs, when the league's top teams vie to get into the Super Bowl championship game. Then, as many overtime periods as needed are played until one team scores. (The longest game in NFL history, an AFC Divisional Playoff Game between the Miami Dolphins and the Kansas City Chiefs, lasted well into the second over-

The quarterback always must be conscious of the 45-second clock, which is independent of the scoreboard clock and is reset at the end of each play.

time, 82 minutes and 40 seconds in all; Miami won 27-24.)

The *game clock* on the scoreboard is the official clock; it counts down the time remaining in each quarter. If the scoreboard clock malfunctions, the official called the "line judge" takes over timing the game. In addition to the game clock, offensive teams must deal with the independent *45-second clock*. Each offensive play must begin within 45 seconds of the preceding play or the offense is penalized for "delay of game."

Each team is allowed to call three 1-minute, 50-second *time outs* during each half. Officials also can call time outs whenever necessary to assess penalties, measure yardage, tend to injured players, or inform both teams when there are two minutes remaining in the second and fourth quarters of the game (called the "two-minute warning").

Moving the Ball

All progress in a football game is measured in yards. The offensive team tries to get as much "yardage" (as many yards) as it can on every play. The defensive team tries to stop the offensive team and make it lose yardage. When a team goes on the offensive it not only gets *possession of the ball*, it gets a set of four *downs*, or chances, in which to gain 10 yards. If the offensive team successfully moves the ball 10 or more yards, it earns another set of four downs. If it fails to gain 10 yards, it loses possession of the ball. The situation on the field at the time of each play is expressed in both down number and distance (total yards needed to make a first down on that particular play). For example, when a team first gets possession of the ball, it has "first-and-10," or first down and 10 yards to go for a new first down. Or a team could be facing a "third-and-two" situation, meaning it is on its third down of the series and needs to gain two more yards to make a new first down. Third down usually is the make-or-break down. If the offense doesn't make the necessary yardage, it generally will *punt* (kick) the ball away to the other team on fourth down rather than risk not getting the needed yardage and losing the ball where its unsuccessful play was stopped. When a team gets inside its opponent's 10-yard line, the language of down and distance changes slightly. If the offense, for example, gets to its opponent's 9-yard line for a first down, the situation it then faces is said to be "*first and goal.*" In other words, it has a first down and less than 10 yards to go for a touchdown.

WAYS TO MOVE THE BALL

Run: Technically, any offensive player can carry the ball, but it is the running backs who almost always do it. The quarterback, the wide receivers, and the tight end occasionally run with the ball.

Forward Pass: Though any offensive player can throw a pass, the quarterback does it most of the time. Only certain offensive players are eligible to catch a pass—the wide receivers, the running backs, the tight end, and, on rare trick plays, the quarterback.

Lateral Pass: A ball carrier may *lateral* (toss the ball sideways or backwards) to a teammate in an effort to continue a play. If the teammate doesn't catch the ball, it is considered a "free ball" and can be recovered by the defense.

Interception: Any defensive player can make an *interception* (catch a pass intended for an offensive player) and run with the ball.

Fumble: Any defensive player can recover and advance a *fumbled* (dropped after having possession) ball. Specific rules apply to when an offensive player can advance a fumble.

Kick Return: The *receiving team* (the team to which the ball is kicked or punted) "returns" the ball as far as it can.

Blocked Punt or Field Goal: If the defense blocks a punt or field-goal attempt, it can recover and advance the ball.

Penalty: Yardage can be gained or lost by penalty assessment. Likewise, downs can be lost or replayed, or automatic first downs gained by penalty.

John McDonough

Passes are riskier than running plays, but have the potential to gain more yardage. In general, the more wide-open an offense is, the more passes it will throw; the more conservative a team is, the more running plays it will use. Most NFL teams, though, favor an offensive attack with an equal balance of passes and runs.

Rob Brown

Using a *pitchout* (*photo, left*), instead of a handoff, is a good way for the quarterback to get the ball to a running back who is going to run "wide" (outside). A *lateral* is similar to a pitchout, but usually takes place between two players who are farther downfield or on kick or interception return plays.

Scoring

Touchdown

A touchdown is the biggest single score in a football game. It is worth six points, and it allows the scoring team an opportunity to attempt an *extra point*. To score a touchdown, the ball must be carried across the goal line into the end zone, "breaking the vertical plane of the goal," or caught in the end zone, or a fumble recovered in the end zone, or an untouched kickoff recovered in the end zone by the kicking team. Touchdowns usually are scored by the team on offense, but they also can be scored by defenders returning intercepted passes, running with recovered fumbles or blocked kicks, and by punt and kick returners.

Extra Point

Also called "point after touchdown," "PAT," or "conversion," the extra-point play immediately follows a touchdown. The ball is placed on the 2-yard line. The extra point, worth one point, almost always is kicked by the placekicker. To score, the extra-point kick must go through the uprights of the goal post and over the crossbar. If a kick is blocked by the defense, the ball is dead and cannot be advanced by the offense. Though a relatively short kick for an NFL placekicker, extra-point tries are not automatic. If a team chooses to run or pass for an extra point, the same rules as for scoring a touchdown apply, although only one point is scored.

Field Goal

Field goals are worth three points and often are the deciding plays in the last seconds of close games. They can be attempted from anywhere on the field and on any down, but generally are kicked from inside the defense's 45-yard line on fourth down. For a field goal to be "good," the placekicker must kick the ball through the goal-post uprights and over the crossbar in the same manner as an extra-point kick. Defenses also try to block field goals. If they succeed, they not only can recover the ball and gain possession of it there, they can run back the ball and score. When computing how far a field-goal attempt must travel, remember that the goal posts are 10 yards deep in the end zone, and that the ball is kicked from approximately seven yards behind the actual line of scrimmage. So a field-goal try snapped from the 30-yard line actually is a 47-yard attempt. (The longest field goal in NFL history was 63 yards.) If a field-goal attempt from outside the 20-yard line is missed, the defensive team gets possession of the ball at the point from which the ball was snapped. If a field-goal attempt from inside the 20 is missed, the other team gets the ball at its own 20.

Safety

A rarity, a safety is worth two points. (It has no connection with the player position of the same name.) The most common way of scoring a safety occurs when the defense tackles an offensive ball carrier behind his own goal line. A safety also is scored by the defensive team when an offensive player is called for a penalty behind his own goal line, or if the ball is snapped, carried, or fumbled out of bounds in the end zone.

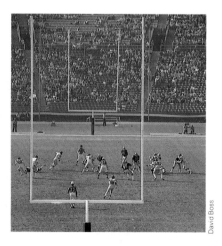

The goal posts are the targets on field-goal and extra-point plays. Gold in color, goal posts have ribbons at the tops of their uprights to aid kickers in determining wind strength and direction.

David Boss

The goal line is not just a line on the field, it represents a plane extending vertically from the stripe on the field. To score, a player only has to break *the plane of the goal* with the ball. For example, a running back who dives toward the end zone and crosses the plane of the goal line in the air has scored, even if he is pushed back to the 1-yard line. A player also can score by reaching with the ball to break the goal plane, as long as the ball is in his possession and he is not yet whistled *down* by the officials.

Mickey Elliot

Offenses must be very careful when they have the ball close to their own goal line. In such situations, they generally use low-risk plays, such as inside runs, until they get further up the field. Pass plays are particularly dangerous, because the quarterback must drop back into the end zone where he risks getting *sacked* for a safety (*photo, left*).

Bill Cummings

Officials

There is a third team on the field at every NFL game. Along with the two competing teams, there is a team of seven *officials* whose job it is to enforce the rules, signal and assess penalties, and make judgment calls about such things as ball possession and whether a player is in or out of bounds. Officials wear their own uniforms—black-and-white striped shirts—and are involved in some way in every play in the game, from the opening coin toss to determine which team will kick off and which will receive, to shooting the final gun to signal the end of the game. The head of the officials is the referee. He wears a white hat and has final authority in close calls. The other officials are the umpire, head linesman, line judge, back judge, side judge, and field judge. Each is responsible for a certain area of the field and portion of play, and can call a penalty whenever he sees an infraction of the rules. Officials call penalties in two ways. They either blow their whistles to stop play, or throw a yellow "penalty marker" in the air, or both. Some plays are stopped immediately when a penalty is signaled, while other plays are allowed to continue to their conclusion before any assessments are made.

Man ty Rubio

Attending the head linesman from the sideline is a two-man chain crew (or "chain gang") that moves the sideline markers (a length of chain exactly 10 yards long between two poles, used to measure for first downs) after each play, and another person who carries and changes the down indicator (a pole with large flip-cards on top numbered 1-2-3-4) to correspond to the down being played.

Instant Replay

In 1986, the NFL began using televised instant replay to help in making close calls. Two specially designated people man a television monitor and tape replay machine in the broadcast booth. If a possession, touchdown, or boundary call is disputed or is too close for the officials on the field to call with absolute certainty, the "replay official" and his "facilitator" quickly view the television footage from all available camera angles. If there is clear visual evidence that a call is in error, the replay official can reverse it. The replay official cannot rule on penalty calls.

Official Signals

When something happens on the field that involves the officials, the referee communicates what has happened to fans via a microphone and a set of hand signals. Here are the most common official signals:

Time out	Touchdown, field goal, extra point	Personal foul	Illegal use of hands
Offside or encroaching	Holding	Illegal motion	First down
Illegal contact	Delay of game	Pass interference	Incomplete pass, penalty refused, missed kick

Coaches

Every NFL team has a group of coaches (the "coaching staff") who teach the players, help them develop their talents, and guide the team on the field. The man in absolute control of the team is the *head coach*. He makes the ultimate decisions about personnel, runs practices, and directs the team's play. The head coach also decides how many *assistant coaches* he needs, and divides the day-to-day coaching responsibilities among them. Most NFL teams have assistant coaches in charge of the overall offensive and defensive units ("offensive coordinator" and "defensive coordinator"), coaches in charge of the various player position groups (such as linebackers, defensive backs, offensive linemen, and receivers), and specialized coaches for strength training and conditioning. Teams also have *trainers* to assist players in prevention, treatment, and rehabilitation of injuries, and equipment managers to keep the players properly dressed for action. In July, prior to the beginning of each NFL season, every NFL team runs a "training camp." At these "preseason" training camps, players compete for spots on the team and hone their skills under the watchful eyes of the coaches. By September and the beginning of the "regular season," each team's roster has been trimmed down to the allotted 45 men, from which the 11-man offensive, defensive, and special teams units are organized. The coaches work hard preparing for each

game, analyzing the strengths and weaknesses of the upcoming opponent and formulating a strategic *game plan* made up of the plays and defenses they think will work best. During a game, between plays, during time outs, and at halftime, the coaches adjust the game plan and make player substitutions. The head coach, or one of his coordinators, sends in the offensive plays to the quarterback on the field, and the defensive alignments to the defensive signal caller. How well the coaches have prepared the team before the game, and how well they make adjustments to the action on the field during the game, often mean the difference between victory and defeat.

NFL coaches consider themselves to be teachers. Though the basics of football are easily understood, at the professional level it is an incredibly complex game. Coaches use traditional teaching methods as well as tools such as computers and videotape to help players learn.

14

Players go through grueling drills at training camp and at daily practice sessions during the season. The various units of the team practice separately, then get together to "scrimmage" (a simulated game in which one side imitates the offense or defense of an upcoming opponent).

While one unit is on the field during a game, the other unit is on the sideline discussing strategy with the coaches. They are aided by the tactical input of assistant coaches stationed high in the press box, who communicate play-by-play intelligence via telephone headsets.

Equipment

Football is a hard-hitting contact sport. To protect themselves, and each other, players wear a helmet and a full complement of "pads" under their uniform jerseys and pants. The NFL has standards that require all players to wear the same basic padding. Any special padding or brace worn by a player must be approved by the umpire before a game. In addition to their equipment, by league rule all players must have their ankles taped before practice or a game. NFL teams have two sets of uniforms, one to wear in home games (usually with a colored jersey), and one to wear in away games (usually with a white jersey). Each player's number appears on the front, back, and sleeves of his jersey; his name appears on the back.

Shoulder Pads

Players at various positions wear different kinds of shoulder pads. In general, the more contact the position requires, the bigger the pads.

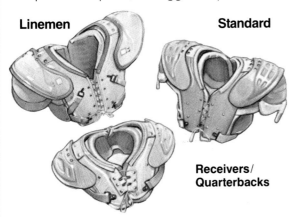

Linemen

Standard

Receivers/ Quarterbacks

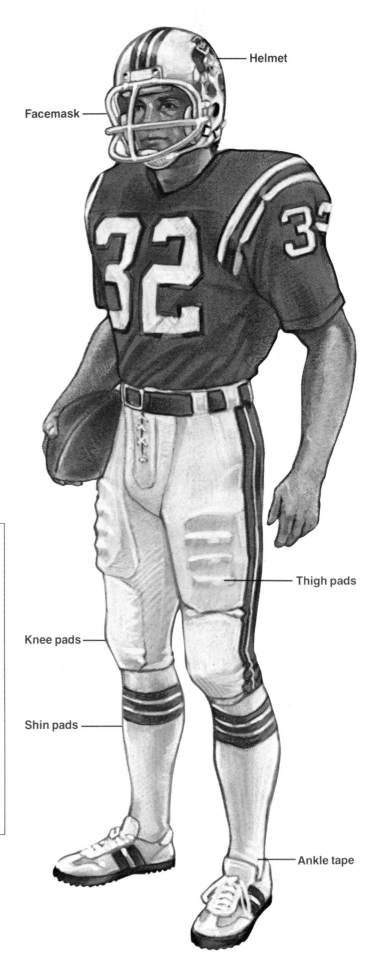

Helmet

Facemask

Thigh pads

Knee pads

Shin pads

Ankle tape

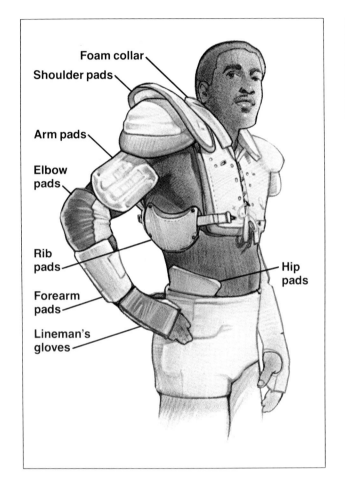

Foam collar
Shoulder pads
Arm pads
Elbow pads
Rib pads
Forearm pads
Lineman's gloves
Hip pads

Helmets

Helmets are custom-fit to the individual player, and lined with energy-absorbing internal materials, such as foam padding, or air- or liquid-filled cells. Each helmet is fitted with a facemask designed to provide maximum protection and visibility; some even have clear-plastic eye-shields.

Shoes

Specialized shoes are worn to match specific playing surfaces and field conditions. For playing on artificial turf, the shoes worn have small rubber nubs, which provide better traction on the carpet-like surface. On grass fields, players wear cleats of interchangeable lengths.

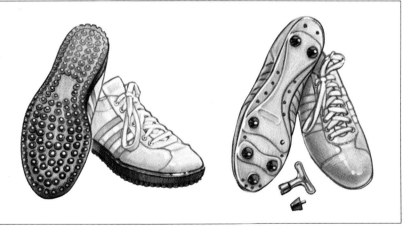

Quarterback

The quarterback is the leader of the offense, the player who makes things happen. In the *huddle* (the brief gathering between plays), the quarterback calls the play and assigns each player a specific role. At the beginning of each offensive play, when his teammates line up in their various positions, the quarterback stands behind the center and shouts out coded signals. On the correct code word, the ball is *snapped* to the quarterback, who then does one of three things: (1) hands or pitches the ball to a running back; (2) *passes* (throws) the ball down the field to one of his receivers; or (3) runs with the ball himself. Some quarterbacks are better runners than others; a good running quarterback adds an extra dimension to the offense and puts added pressure on the defense. On passing plays, the quarterback must take the snap, *drop back* from the line of scrimmage into the protective *pocket* formed by his blockers or *roll out* toward the sideline, avoid the defensive players (*pass rushers*) coming after him, find a free receiver, and accurately throw the ball to him—all in from two to four seconds. The quarterback also must be able to *read* the defense, determining from the positions of the defensive players what the defense is going to do. If, at the line of scrimmage, the quarterback thinks that the play he has called in the huddle will be stopped by the defense, he can change the play by calling an *audible* (a new play designated by code words).

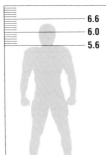

Average Size

A big, strong, mobile quarterback is better able to fend off and avoid pass rushers.

Height: 6 feet 4 inches
Weight: 210 pounds

6.6
6.0
5.6

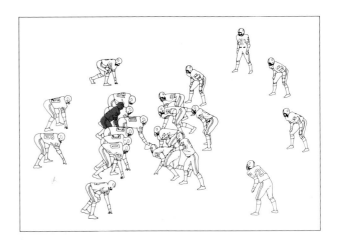

Gin Ellis

On passing downs, some teams have their quarterback take the snap standing in the backfield, three to four yards behind the center. Called the "Shotgun" or "Spread" formation, this set allows the quarterback more time to pick out a receiver and avoid the pass rush. Occasionally, teams will run out of the Shotgun formation.

Running Backs

Running backs are all-purpose offensive players. Their primary responsibility is to take a *handoff* or *pitchout* (an underhand toss) from the quarterback and run with it as far as they can before being tackled. But running backs also can be pass receivers, usually on short-range pass plays, and often function as blockers for their backfield mates. Some running backs even are good passers. There are two basic classifications of running backs. *Halfbacks* can be small and quick or strong and athletic. *Fullbacks* are big, powerful runners who block more than they carry the ball. Halfbacks have speed and generally run to the *outside* (around the end of the line). Fullbacks rush *inside*, between the two tackles. They often carry the ball in short-yardage situations (when the team needs fewer than three yards to make a first down), or when the ball is near the goal line. Both halfbacks and fullbacks must be able to move with the snap of the ball, follow the blockers leading them through the line, find some "daylight" (running room), and hold on to the ball and not *fumble* (lose possession) when being tackled. Some NFL teams use two running backs set behind the quarterback in the *backfield* (the area immediately behind the offensive line). Other teams use only one running back. Most, however, rotate different running backs into the game, singly or in combination, depending on the situation.

When a halfback gets outside around the end of the line, he is at his most dangerous. He then turns upfield and shifts into high gear, picking up blockers and trying to outrun the deep defenders.

George Rose

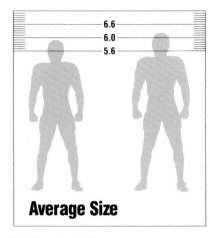

Average Size

Halfback *(left)*
   Height: 5 feet 11 inches
   Weight: 190 pounds
Fullback *(right)*
   Height: 6 feet 2 inches
   Weight: 225 pounds

Fullbacks carry the ball on inside runs. Each running play calls for the running back to go through a specific hole that the blocking scheme is designed to open. If the blocking fails to open the designated hole, the runner must improvise, either "cutting back" (reversing his field), running to the outside, or trying to ram through the line.

Michael Zagaris

21

Wide Receivers

Wide receivers are pass-catching specialists. They generally are the fastest men on the team and come in all sizes. They are expert at making sharp-angled turns while running at full speed and excel at racing down the field once they have caught the ball. On a pass play, as soon as the ball is snapped, the wide receivers begin to run their *pass patterns*, or specific routes that will take them to a designated area of the field. The object is to elude the defenders assigned to *cover* (or watch) them and get *open* (in the clear). The quarterback always will try to pass the ball to the open receiver. Wide receivers catch passes all over the field: short passes near the line of scrimmage, medium-range passes "over the middle" or near the sidelines, and long passes, called "bombs," which can be the most exciting plays of a game and often go for touchdowns. One wide receiver is positioned on the line of scrimmage, usually split out away from the linemen. Another wide receiver, actually a fourth member of the backfield, is lined up a yard behind the line of scrimmage, split to the outside.

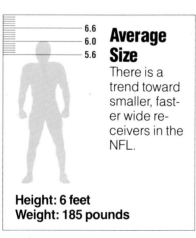

Average Size

There is a trend toward smaller, faster wide receivers in the NFL.

Height: 6 feet
Weight: 185 pounds

6.6
6.0
5.6

Michael Minardi

Wide receivers work closely with their quarterbacks on the timing and routes of pass patterns. On some pass plays, the quarterback throws the ball to a specific spot on the field before his receiver even has turned around or made his cut. From practice, the quarterback knows exactly where the receiver should be. Pass receivers have an advantage over a defender because they know the route they will run and the defender doesn't. Even if the receiver isn't going to get the pass, he runs his route to attract defenders away from the ball.

Pass Patterns

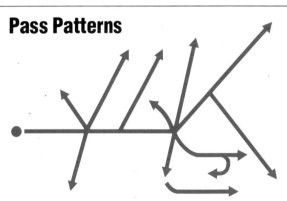

All pass receivers run *pass patterns*, designated routes that are part of the play called in the huddle. Pass patterns have names that indicate the direction in which they are run. For example, "out" patterns go toward the sidelines, "in" patterns toward the middle of the field, and "post" patterns toward the goal post.

Tight End

The tight end is a hard-to-find combination of a wide receiver and a lineman. He must be able to run short-to-medium-range pass patterns, catch the ball, and run with it like a wide receiver. But he also has to have the size and strength to block big defensive linemen and linebackers. Defenses use the placement of the offense's tight end as a key. The side of the offensive line that includes the tight end is called the *strongside*. The side of the line with only a wide receiver and no tight end is called the *weakside*. Because of the extra blocking power the tight end adds, teams generally run to their strongside, but not always; sometimes the tight end is used as a decoy to fool the defense. Also, many teams use two or even three tight ends (removing one or two wide receivers) in short-yardage or goal-line situations, thereby eliminating the strongside/weakside distinction. Having two or more tight ends on the field adds power no matter which direction the team runs without sacrificing receiving ability.

Most teams run to the tight end's side of the line, called the *strongside*. On outside runs, the blocking of the tight end (*number 89 in photo*) is critical, sealing off the defensive end or outside linebacker and preventing the opponent from stopping the play at the line of scrimmage. Occasionally, the tight end will slide off his initial block to become a pass receiver, or go "in motion," running along the line of scrimmage before the ball is snapped. (In the photo at right, wide receiver number 88 is in motion.)

Herb Weitman

Average Size

Speed and blocking ability must be balanced with size in tight ends.

6.6
6.0
5.6

Height: 6 feet 3 inches
Weight: 235

Tackles

Tackles are the big men of the offense, the players who provide protection for their smaller teammates who handle the ball. On every play, the tackles must go head-to-head with defensive linemen, on running plays blocking the defenders so the running backs can get past, and on passing plays keeping the pass rushers away from the quarterback. For men of their size and strength, tackles must have fast reflexes and be quick on their feet. They must be able to fire out of the *set position* (a motionless three-point stance offensive linemen must assume) as soon as the ball is snapped to attack their assigned defender, as well as be skilled masters of the very different techniques of pass protection and run-blocking. Their job is hard, dirty, and exhausting, requiring great discipline and concentration but offering little glamour or recognition. However, without the contributions of tackles, the offense would go nowhere.

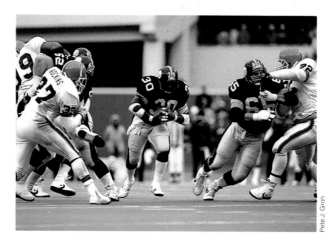

Pete J. Groh

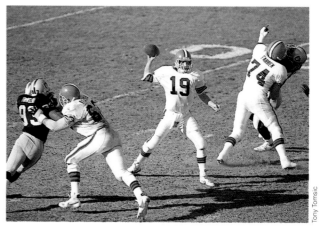

Tony Tomsic

It is the job of the tackles, and all offensive linemen, to open "holes" for the running backs. Depending on the direction of the play and the area of the line through which the running back is going to run, the tackles either block their men in the same direction, or (*photo, above*) opposite directions.

On pass plays, the tackles work in combination with the other offensive linemen to create a protective "pocket" for the quarterback. In pass blocking, the tackles not only must watch the men they are assigned to block, but must be alert for extra pass rushers coming in on a *blitz*.

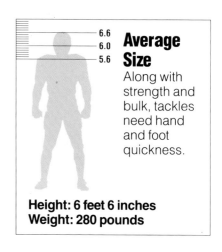

Average Size

Along with strength and bulk, tackles need hand and foot quickness.

6.6
6.0
5.6

Height: 6 feet 6 inches
Weight: 280 pounds

Guards

Guards perform many of the same duties as tackles, but are more mobile. This mobility comes into action on outside running plays, when guards *pull* (leave their positions on the line) to lead a running back downfield. Sometimes guards will pull to fake the defense into thinking a play is going in a certain direction (called "misdirection"). Other times, guards will pull in order to throw a "trap block" on an unsuspecting defender farther down the line. On most inside running plays, it is the guards who must clear out the center of the defense, allowing the ball carrier to slash through the line behind them. Like tackles, guards must be good pass blockers, helping to form the protective *pocket* (wall of blockers) around the quarterback as he looks downfield for a receiver. When the quarterback throws a short pass out to a running back (called a "screen pass"), often it is the responsibility of the guard on that side to slide off his original block and help lead interference.

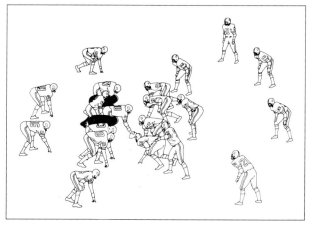

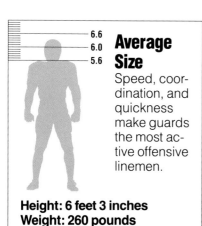

Guards and the other offensive linemen are at a disadvantage when they pass block because the rules allow defenders freer use of their hands. The offensive linemen do have one thing in their favor, though. They know the play and they know on what signal the ball will be snapped.

Pulling guards become formidable lead blockers for running backs on runs to the outside. When a guard pulls, he leaves his position at the snap, runs parallel to the line of scrimmage, then turns upfield once the running back is behind him.

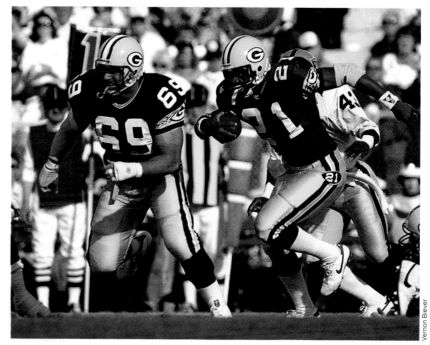

Average Size

6.6
6.0
5.6

Speed, coordination, and quickness make guards the most active offensive linemen.

Height: 6 feet 3 inches
Weight: 260 pounds

Center

The center is the only player who handles the ball on every offensive play. He *snaps* the ball (by passing it backwards between his legs) to the quarterback, to the punter, and to the holder on field-goal and extra-point attempts. The center must be as strong and tough as he is quick and smart. He often has a defender playing directly opposite him, poised to charge at the snap of the ball. So the center must be able to snap the ball, then get his hands up and body set for the impact with the onrushing defender. The anchor of the offensive line, the center's job begins at the end of each offensive play when he huddles the team around the quarterback to call the next play. Once he reaches the line of scrimmage, the center calls out coded signals to the other linemen to help them cope with shifts by the defense. The center's calls tell the other offensive linemen who to block and how to block them.

As soon as the center snaps the ball to the quarterback to begin an offensive play (*photos above*), he must contend with a defensive lineman or linebacker. The center's blocking is crucial on every play—run or pass—because of his central position in the offensive line.

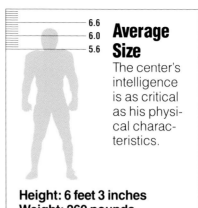

Average Size

The center's intelligence is as critical as his physical characteristics.

6.6
6.0
5.6

Height: 6 feet 3 inches
Weight: 260 pounds

Defensive Ends

Defensive ends fill critical positions on the defensive line. Depending on the defensive alignment, the defensive ends play either straight across from, or slightly to either side of, the offensive tackles. On outside runs, they are the first-line of defense; their job is to stop the ball carrier from turning upfield into the defensive backfield. Defensive ends must be strong enough to fight off a runner's lead blockers and hold their position, then either make the tackle or force the runner to cut back to the inside. Ends also must be fast enough to pursue running backs while run-ning away from their position. On passing plays, defensive ends are key pass rushers. They use their agility and quickness to get by pass blockers and pressure the quarterback from an outside angle, attempting to *sack* (tackle) him or keep him in the pocket where the inside pass rushers can get to him. Because defensive ends often are the tallest men on the team, they rush with their arms up, making the quarterback throw with an obstructed view over their outstretched hands. This often results in tipped, batted, in-tercepted, or incomplete passes.

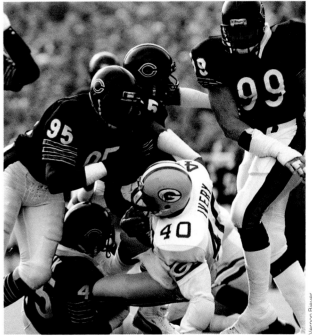

Vernon Biever

Often working in tandem, the defensive ends (*numbers 95 and 99 in photo, right*) try to force running backs into the middle of the field. In that area of the de-fense, runners are easier prey for the linebackers and safeties and are less likely to gain big yardage. The defensive ends have to remain alert no matter how fu-rious the action on the line becomes because of-fenses often initially disguise passing plays to look like runs (called "play-action passes").

Average Size

Defensive ends usually are lankier and faster than their defensive linemates.

6.6
6.0
5.6

Height: 6 feet 5 inches
Weight: 255 pounds

Defensive Tackles

Defensive tackles are the big men who guard the middle of the line, sealing off running holes before running backs can get through them. Defensive tackles also rush the quarterback, either making him hurry his passes or flushing him out of his protective pocket toward the defensive ends. Defensive tackles do not always rush straight at the quarterback. To confuse the offensive blockers, the defensive tackles sometimes will loop around the defensive ends, exchanging rushing lanes. Such maneuvers are called *stunts*. Some teams use two defensive tackles, others only one. When only one defensive tackle is used, he is called the *nose tackle* because he lines up nose-to-nose with the offensive center. Defensive tackles often are the biggest men on the defense; nose tackles are shorter and stockier, with a lower center of gravity to help them hold their ground in the center of the defensive formation.

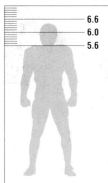

Average Size

For men so big, defensive tackles/ nose tackles exhibit great body control and quickness.

Height: 6 feet 4 inches
Weight: 270 pounds

A quarterback who holds the ball too long as he looks for a receiver risks being sacked (*photo, above*) by an onrushing defensive tackle. Even if the defensive tackle or nose tackle doesn't sack the quarterback, he can pressure the passer (*photo, right*) into a bad or hurried throw, or make him *scramble* out of the pocket.

Linebackers

Linebackers are the most versatile—and volatile—players on the defense, requiring considerable athletic ability, quick reactions, and strategic skills on every play. Their responsibilities vary with each down. On passing plays, linebackers may have to *cover* (watch) a running back coming out of the backfield as a receiver, or protect a *zone* (a specific area of the field). Sometimes they go after the quarterback on a surprise pass rush called a *blitz*. On runs, they must pursue and tackle the ball carrier. And between plays, it usually is a linebacker who calls the signals in the defensive huddle and directs defensive shifts prior to the snap of the ball. Depending on the team and the situation, there generally are either three or four linebackers in the game who change their positions from standing a few yards off the line of scrimmage, to just behind the defensive linemen, to being on the line of scrimmage.

Linebackers use the element of surprise to pressure quarterbacks, who do not know if the linebacker will be rushing on a blitz (*photo, left*) or dropping back into pass coverage. On runs (*photo, above*), linebackers must anticipate the direction of the play and lead the pursuit of the ball carrier.

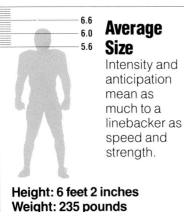

6.6	
6.0	**Average**
5.6	**Size**

Average Size
Intensity and anticipation mean as much to a linebacker as speed and strength.

Height: 6 feet 2 inches
Weight: 235 pounds

Cornerbacks

Cornerbacks combine speed and power in a compact package. They must be able to keep up with the fastest receivers in pass coverage, yet be strong enough to bring down big, powerful running backs head-on. Cornerbacks must be smart and quick, able to match strides with fleet pass receivers man-to-man and not be taken in by the receiver's fakes during his pass pattern. Depending on the defensive play called, cornerbacks either will be guarding a specific zone on the field (*a zone defense*), or a specific receiver (called *man-to-man* coverage). Once the ball is in the air, it is the cornerback's job either to break up the pass play, intercept the ball, or tackle the receiver if the catch is made. Along with the defensive ends, cornerbacks have the responsibility of protecting the wide part of the field. They must instantaneously be able to recognize a running play as it develops, leave the receiver they are covering, then come up fast toward the line of scrimmage and fight past any lead blockers to get to the ball carrier. Once a runner gets into the *defensive secondary* (the area behind the linebackers), the cornerbacks must take control and stop the play.

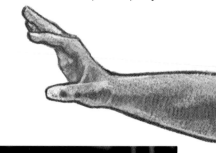

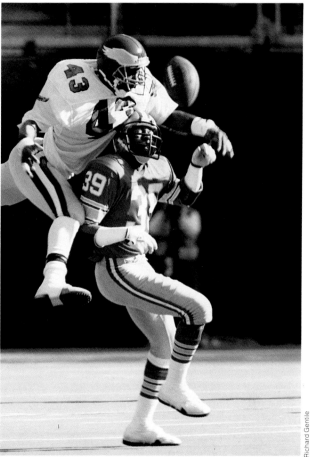

Timing is important when a cornerback breaks up a pass play and knocks the ball away. He risks a costly pass interference penalty if he hits the receiver before the receiver touches the ball, though both receiver and defender have an equal right to catch the ball.

Richard Gentile

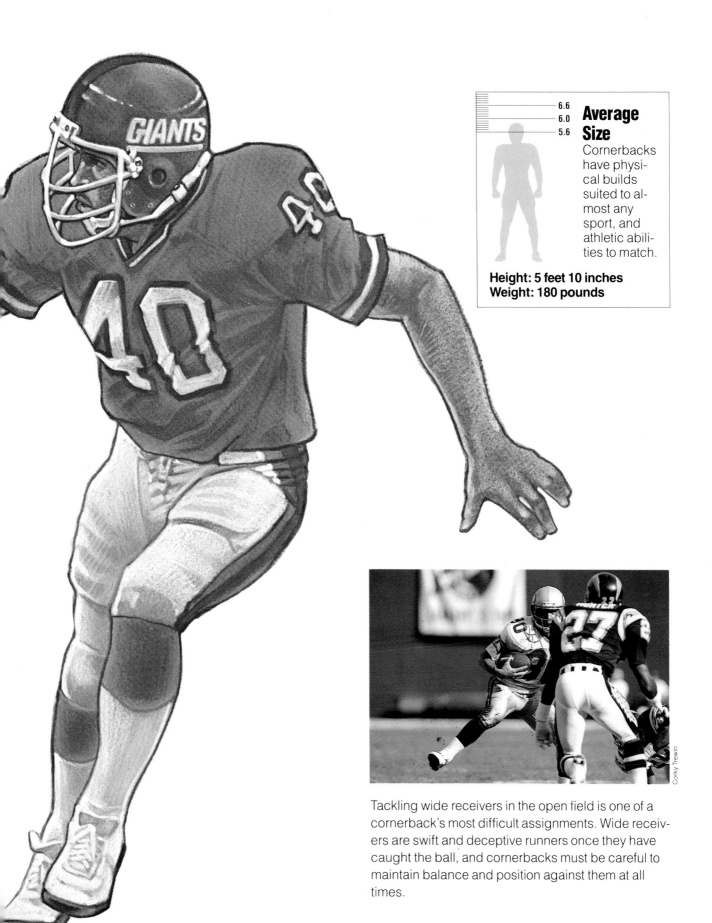

Average Size

6.6
6.0
5.6

Cornerbacks have physical builds suited to almost any sport, and athletic abilities to match.

Height: 5 feet 10 inches
Weight: 180 pounds

Tackling wide receivers in the open field is one of a cornerback's most difficult assignments. Wide receivers are swift and deceptive runners once they have caught the ball, and cornerbacks must be careful to maintain balance and position against them at all times.

Corky Trewin

Safeties

There are two safeties in the defensive secondary, the *strong safety* and the *free safety*. The strong safety usually lines up on the same side of the field as the offense's tight end and generally is a sure tackler. The free safety usually plays the ball and is available to help the other defenders in pass coverage. He also is the key man on a gambling pass rush called a *safety blitz*. The safeties' main responsibility is pass defense. On long passes, a safety is the only player between a receiver and a touchdown. On long runs, the safety may be the last defender with a chance to tackle the ball carrier or knock him out of bounds. Safeties often are the defense's leading tacklers; pound-for-pound, they can be the hardest hitters on the team.

George Rose

A "safety blitz" is not called often, but it can be a devastating defensive play to sack or unnerve the quarterback.

The players in the defensive secondary work as a unit to protect the deep zones. On critical downs or certain passing situations, the defense may assign two players to cover the most dangerous receivers (called "double coverage"). The action in the defensive secondary often is a direct reflection of the action on the line of scrimmage. If the pass rushers do their job well, forcing the quarterback into an ill-advised or poorly placed throw, an interception (*photo, left*) often is the result.

Arthur Anderson

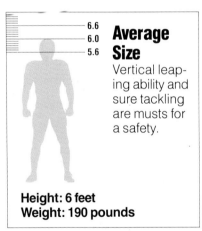

Average Size

Vertical leaping ability and sure tackling are musts for a safety.

6.6
6.0
5.6

Height: 6 feet
Weight: 190 pounds

Kickers

Punter

Kickers are specialists who are used in specific, often high-pressure, situations. There are two types of kickers on most teams, the *punter* and the *placekicker*. The punter comes into the game almost exclusively on fourth down, when the offense thinks it cannot make, or should not try for, a first down. The decision then is made to punt the ball, or kick it away, to the other team. In most cases, the punter wants to kick the ball as far as he can toward his opponent's goal line, giving the other team possession of the ball with poor field position. In addition to distance, punters also are concerned with the height of their kicks and how long the ball stays in the air (called "hang time"); the longer a punt takes to come down, the more time the punt-coverage team has to get downfield under it and limit the return. But punters require more than just a strong and limber leg. On some punt plays, they must be able to direct their kicks away from dangerous kick returners. On others, usually when kicking from near

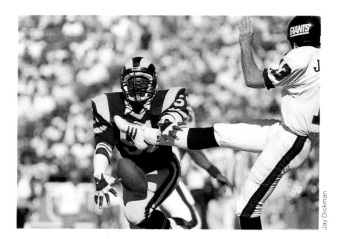

Most punters kick the ball too quickly for it to be blocked. But an errant snap from the center or an extra step on the punter's part can give a punt rusher that extra fraction of a second he needs to get to the ball. Blocked punts always are costly for the kicking team, and sometimes disastrous.

Pete J. Groh

There's chaotic action on every field goal or extra-point play. The holder must catch the long snap and place it down properly, the rushers streak around the end as the kicker steps into the ball, the blockers fire out, and the defensive linemen leap with their hands up to block the soaring kick.

midfield, they try to angle the ball out of bounds near the goal line to pin the other team against its own end zone. Place-kickers are responsible for the *kickoffs* that begin each half and follow touch-downs and field goals. On kickoffs, the ball is placed upright on a "kicking tee" on the kicking team's 35-yard line. On *point-after-touchdown* plays (also called "extra point" or "conversion" plays) and *field-goal* attempts, placekickers always work with a *holder*, who takes the long snap from center and places the ball down in kicking position about seven yards behind the line of scrimmage. Most NFL placekickers kick the ball from the side, soccer-style. On extra-point plays, the ball is snapped from the 2-yard line. Field goals can be attempted from anywhere on the field, but rarely are tried from beyond the defense's 45-yard line.

**Placekicker
and Holder**

Special Teams

Along with the offensive and defensive units of each team, there is another 11-man unit called the *special teams* that comes into the game on kickoffs, punts, field goals, and extra points. The responsibilities of the special teams vary as follows with the situation:

Kickoffs: The special teams unit of the *kicking team* tries to get downfield as quickly as possible and minimize the kick return of the receiving team, or make the returner fumble the ball. The goal of the special teams unit of the *receiving team* is to form a wedge of blockers in front of the kick or punt returner so he can gain as much yardage as he can on his "runback." If a kicking team is behind late in the game, it may try an *onside kick*, a risky, short kickoff that can be recovered by either team after it has traveled 10 yards. In such a case, the job of the receiving team is to cover the ball immediately and prevent the kicking team from getting it.

Punts: The job of the *kicking team's* special teams unit on a punt is the same as on a kickoff. For the *receiving team's* special teams unit there sometimes is an added goal—the linemen try to break through the line and block the punt. If they are unsuccessful or there was no punt block on, they block the kicking team's linemen to slow their pursuit of the kick returner, then drop back downfield and form a blocking wall for the runback.

Field Goals and Extra Points: The special teams unit of the *kicking team* tries to block the players from the defense and protect the kicker and holder. The *defensive* special teams players rush the kicker and holder in order to make the holder fumble or misplace the snap, hurry the kicker so that his kick misses, or block the kick altogether.

George Gojkovich

The special teams unit is made up of offensive and defensive players and kickers. Kickoffs (*photo above*), kick and punt returns, and field goal- and extra-point plays are practiced thoroughly; they are critical plays on which many games have turned.

Football Dictionary

audible: A change in plays shouted in code by the quarterback at the line of scrimmage.

backfield: The area behind the offensive line of scrimmage where the quarterback and running backs stand. The defensive secondary is called the "defensive backfield."

blitz: A pass rush by one or more linebackers, and/or a defensive back.

block: 1. To get in the way of an opponent so that he cannot get to the ball carrier. 2. To knock down a punt, field-goal, or extra-point kick.

bomb: A long pass.

chain crew: The three men on the sideline who assist with the measuring chain and down marker.

clipping: An illegal block caused by throwing the body across the back of an opponent. Clipping usually occurs downfield on punt, kickoff, and interception plays.

complete pass: A pass caught by the offense. Also called a "completion."

coverage: 1. Pass defense. 2. Movement of a kicking team downfield after a kick.

crossbar: The horizontal bar of a goal post over which a field-goal or extra-point kick must go. The crossbar is 10 feet above the ground.

dead ball: When the ball no longer can be advanced, it is whistled "dead" by the officials.

defense: 1. The team without the ball. 2. The tactics of that team.

defensive backs: The men who play in the defensive secondary—the cornerbacks and safeties.

double coverage: Two defensive players covering one receiver.

down: 1. An offensive play; the offense gets four *downs*, or chances—numbered first to fourth—to gain 10 yards and earn a *first down*, or the right to another four-down sequence. 2. When a ball carrier is tackled, his knee touches the ground, or his forward progress is stopped he is con-sidered *down* and the play ends. 3. On a punt, the kicking team may touch the ball and *down* it at the spot it is touched, ending the play. On a kickoff, the receiving team may *down* the ball in the end zone for a touchback by indicating the kick will not be returned. The ball then is brought out to the 20-yard line.

drop back: 1. The backward motion of a quarterback as he moves into the backfield to pass. 2. The backward motion of a linebacker as he goes into pass coverage.

end lines: The end boundaries of the field, parallel to and 10 yards behind the goal lines.

end zone: The 10-yard-deep area behind the goal line. The ball must be carried into the end zone to score a touchdown.

extra point: A one-point play allowed a team after it scores a touchdown. The ball most often is kicked, and must go over the crossbar, but it can be passed or run into the end zone, too. Also called the "point-after-touchdown" (PAT) or "conversion."

fair catch: An unhindered catch of a punt or a kickoff that the kick returner signals by raising his arm over his head before he catches the ball. A fair catch cannot be advanced.

field goal: A scoring kick worth three points that may be attempted from anywhere on the field. It must go through the goal post's uprights and over the crossbar.

45-second clock: A clock, separate from the official game clock, that counts down the 45 seconds allowed the offense to get off a play.

formation: The alignments of offensive or defensive players on a play.

free ball: A loose ball that can be covered by either team.

fumble: Loss of possession of the football by the ball carrier, handler, or passer.

game plan: The strategy and plays chosen for a specific game against a specific opponent.

goal line: The line separating the end zone and the field (at both ends of the field) that ball carriers must cross to score a touchdown or an extra point.

goal post: The structures centered at the back of the end zone on either end of the field. They are used as the targets for field-goal and extra-point kickers. The goal post crossbar is 10 feet high, and the two uprights each are 40 feet high.

half: A 30-minute playing period made up of two 15-minute quarters. A game has a first and second half.

halftime: A 15-minute break between the second and third quarters of a game.

handoff: The act of giving the ball to another player. The quarterback most often hands off to a running back.

hang time: The amount of time a punt stays in the air.

hashmarks: Field markings at one-yard intervals roughly lined up with the goal-post uprights.

holding: A penalty, most often called on offensive linemen, for illegally grabbing or grasping another player.

hole: The space opened by blockers for a runner.

huddle: A brief gathering for play calling by the offense and defense between plays.

incomplete pass: A pass that is not caught. Also called an "incompletion."

inside: The area between the two tackles where running plays can be directed.

interception: When a defensive player catches a pass intended for the offensive player.

interference: A penalty called when either an offensive or defensive player interferes with another player's opportunity to catch a pass.

lateral: A sideways or backwards toss of the ball to another player.

line of scrimmage: The imaginary line, one ball-length wide, running through the ball, from one side of the field to the other. Teams face each other across the line of scrimmage at the beginning of each offensive play.

man-to-man: A type of pass defense in which defensive players each cover one specific pass receiver, as opposed to guarding specific zones.

misdirection: A running play that gives the appearance of going one direction, but actually goes the other.

motion: The lateral movement of one running back or receiver before the snap of the ball.

offense: 1. The team with the ball. 2. The tactics of that team.

offside: A penalty called when a player is across the line of scrimmage at the time the ball is snapped.

onside kick: A short kickoff that carries just beyond the required 10 yards to allow the kicking team a chance to recover the live ball.

outside: The area outside the two tackles where running plays can be directed.

overtime: An extra period that is played if a game ends in a tie.

pass: To throw the ball forward to another player. The quarterback generally passes the ball. The ball can be passed forward only once on any play.

pass pattern: The route a receiver runs on his way to catch a pass.

pass rush: The defensive charge to sack or pressure the quarterback as he attempts to pass.

penalty: An assessment of either yardage or loss of down, or both, for breaking the rules.

penalty marker: The yellow handkerchief thrown by officials to signal a penalty. Also called a *flag*.

pitchout: An underhand toss, usually from a quarterback to a running back. Also called a "pitch."

plane of the goal: The plane extending upward from the goal line that must be broken by a player in possession of the ball to score.

play action: Pass plays in which the quarterback first fakes a handoff to a running back, then passes.

pocket: The area of protection for a quarterback formed by his blockers.

possession: Control of the ball by an individual or team.

pull: The action of an offensive lineman, usually a guard, who leaves his position to lead a play.

punt: To kick the ball to the other team during a series of downs; most often used on fourth down.

quarter: A 15-minute playing period; four quarters, first through fourth, make up a game.

read: The quarterback's observation of the defensive alignment at the line of scrimmage.

receiver: A player who is eligible to catch, or catches, a pass.

receiving team: The team to which the ball is kicked.

roll out: What a quarterback does as he moves sideways across the backfield to set up a pass (as opposed to moving straight back after the snap).

sack: To tackle a quarterback holding the ball behind the line of scrimmage.

safety: 1. A scoring play worth two points that most often occurs when an offensive ball carrier is tackled in his own end zone. 2. A defensive player position in the defensive secondary; there is a strong safety, who plays to the tight end's side of the field, and a free safety.

scramble: What the quarterback does when he runs to avoid being sacked.

screen pass: A short pass to a running back standing behind a "screen" of blockers.

secondary: The defensive backfield and/or pass-coverage personnel.

set: 1. A formation. 2. A motionless position required of offensive players just prior to the snap of the ball.

shotgun: The formation in which the quarterback takes the snap from center five to seven yards behind the line of scrimmage. Also called the "spread."

sideline: The side boundaries of the field. When the ball carrier crosses the sideline, he is *out of bounds* and play stops.

signals: 1. The number and word codes shouted by the quarterback at the line of scrimmage. Signals also are called by the defense prior to a play, usually by a linebacker. 2. Hand signs made by the referee to indicate which penalty has been called.

snap: The exchange of the ball from the center to the quarterback that begins each offensive play.

snap count: The signal on which the ball will be snapped.

special teams: The offensive and de-

fensive units used on kickoffs, punts, extra points, and field goals.

spike: Action of a player slamming the ball to the ground after scoring.

spot: The placement of the ball by the referee after a play or penalty.

strongside: The side of the offensive formation with the tight end.

stunt: A planned pass rush maneuver by defensive linemen, sometimes including linebackers, in which they loop around each other instead of rushing straight ahead.

tackle: 1. To stop a ball carrier by bringing him to the ground. (Much different than the soccer term "tackle.") 2. The offensive and defensive linemen's positions of the same name.

time out: An interval in which the game clock is stopped. Each team is allowed three one-minute, 50-second time outs per half.

touchback: When a kickoff or punt is whistled dead in the end zone. The ball is put in play on the receiving team's 20-yard line.

touchdown: A scoring play worth six points. The ball must be either carried into, or caught in, the other team's end zone.

two-minute warning: The notification, given to both teams by the officials, that two minutes remain in a half.

uprights: The 40-foot vertical poles of a goal post through which an extra-point or field-goal kick must pass.

weakside: The side of the offensive formation without the tight end.

zone: An assigned area of pass coverage. Also a type of pass defense in which defenders are responsible for these assigned areas.